Rune Stone Journal

For Recording Readings

by

Glenn McWane

Rune Stone Journal
For Recording Readings
Glenn McWane

ISBN - 9780934523707

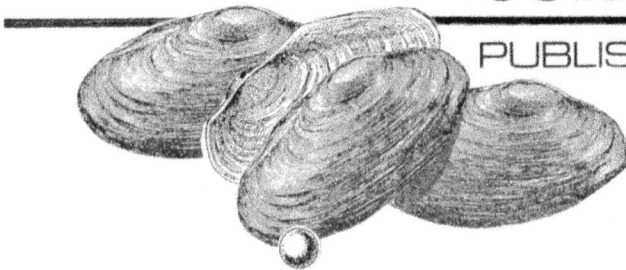

MIDDLE
COAST
PUBLISHING

"Good Books Are Where We Find Our Dreams"

How to Draw

&

Interpret Rune Stones

Creatively

Use this journal to record which runes are drawn and the interpretation of that reading. Days, weeks, months, or even years later, go back to revisit whatever was going on in your life. Most of us have ESP, but Western culture discourages using it. As a result we haven't used it in so long that any clairvoyant ability is hidden in the recesses of our mind, rusting away from disuse. While we may no longer need intuition to sense the presence of a prowling saber-toothed tiger, if we had the benefit of it, we could focus that psychic energy on how to best approach a grumbling life's partner, a difficult co-worker, or make a sound business decision. Naturally, when ESP does breaks through, it's inconsistent, inaccurate-and hard to trust. The good news is reading runes exercises intuition muscles. So naturally it follows, over time, intuition becomes more consistent and reliable.

Rune Stones and Their Meanings

The original runic alphabet comprises 24-letters. At least it did until 1983 when Ralph H. Bloom added a 25th rune in his **Book of Runes**, published by St. Martin's Press. Blum's book has been in print for nearly 40-years! A blank rune stone, dubbed by Blum to be Odin's Rune, is said to symbolize the unknown, something not meant to be known at this time. So in other words, an energy form unfolding before our very eyes.

Juxtaposing this modern rune against mythology, it's interesting to note that the Norse God , Odin is said to have sacrificed one of his eyes so that he might see, he might know, everything happening in the mortal world. So naturally it follows, when this particular rune is drawn, it suggests that one ought to let go, to put trust in the future.

Aett is the Ancient Norse word for Alphabet

As a matter of record, the traditional runic alphabet, the oldest form of the runic alphabets, was the indigenous alphabet of the ancient Germanic tribes prior to adaptation of the Latin alphabet. Ancient Elder Futhark rather neatly divides itself into 3-equal parts. Each one of these three Aetts is comprised of eight-different rune stones, for a total of 24-glyphs. These three Aetts are individually denominated as:

Freyr's Aett
Heimdall's Aett
Haeg's Aett

In general, **Freyr's Aett** represents the ubiquitous cycle of life and all of its changes. These eight runes are illustrated by glyphs for: Wealth, abundance, an exchange of information and intensity of being. Common interpretations include the finding of stability in the corporal world as well as the acquisition of worldly possessions.

In general, the grouping of **Heimdall's Aett** runes relate to obstacles standing in one's path, fate, a copious quantity of something. In general, drawing of these runes portends an expansion in maturity and growth.

The **Haeg's Aett** group of rune stones relate to clairvoyance, the genesis of something new, an inheritance, or a right of possession. They portend a developing deepness of spirituality or consciousness.

FREYR'S AETT

In Norse mythology, Freyr presides over peace, rain and sunshine, as well as fertility of soil and womb. He is the son of the Sea God Njörd.

Fehu represents pending affluence, treasure won in battle, or earned income. It represents a streak of good luck and reflects notions, beliefs, concepts or the seed of an idea. It relates to social success.

When a rune stone is drawn inverted, which is to say upside down, it is considered to be *merkstave*, Merkstave literally means dark stick, implying a dark meaning. A merkstave is not necessarily meant to be interpreted as the opposite its primary meaning. Instead, the interpretation should usually denote a more negative connotation.

Merkstave – An inverted Fehu points a finger at loss. Which could manifest in loss of personal possessions, money, stature, self-esteem or in some life struggle.

Uruz - Ox

Uruz, represents the wild bull and all of his considerable strength and endurance. This as in hard work, perseverance, motivation, and a persistent determination. Uruz indicates a time of substantial energy, fleetness of foot and the enjoyment of good mental and physical health. It shows amplified power and masculinity.

Merkstave – When inverted, Uruz indicates the loss of health (mental or physical), reduced stamina, obstruction, subservience, or a misguided attempt.

7

Thurisaz - Mallet/Giant

Thurisaz represents Thor's hammer, or a giant. As such, this Jovian symbol represents a powerful direction of energy directed either towards destruction, or held close in defense. In other words, great conflict. This could be cathartic, cleansing and purgative.

Merkstave – Drawn in its reversed position, Thurisaz alludes to being in a defenselessness position, betrayal, duress, spiteful behavior or betrayal.

Ansuz

Ansuz, the rune of communication, refers to the ancestral God Odin and therefor represents a divine message or insight arriving. The rune, like Odin himself, is associated with wisdom, healing, death, royalty, the gallows, knowledge, war, doing battle, victory, sorcery, poetry, frenzied activity.

Merkstave – Alas, Ansuz inverted points its accusing finger at a failure to communicate a web of deceit, misunderstandings and manipulated emotions.

Raidho - Journey,

Raidho indicates a journey and represents a wheel. This rune might portend physical travel or a spiritual voyage. So a holiday in far off lands, moving your abode or an expansion of consciousness. It can also be interpreted as having achieved the right perspective, evolution of the soul and the cycle of life.

Merkstave – Raidhow inverted is quite negative and its interpretation signifies stubbornness, injustice, unreasonableness, incoherence or a disturbance.

Kenaz - Torch

Kenaz - The flame or torch, shines a light on truth and finding your own way. The interpretation can point to some things that was previously unknown, perhaps a mystery or secret, being revealed. It means being are on the true path of enlightenment. It means divine influence, knowledge, imagination, invention, inspiration, vitality, regeneration and energy.

Merkstave - Kenaz inverted warns of incognizance, delusion, being en-mired in a creative rut, false hope, and instability.

Gebo – Gift

ᚷ

Gebo - The rune of gifting, is a decidedly positive symbol representing the possession of bountiful gifts and talents. Or alternatively, it poses the notion that someone soon will confer bountiful blessings, which could be gifts of love or friendship. It also relates to generosity, balance, and positive relationships.

Merkstave - Gebo inverted does not have an inverted meaning.

Wunjo - Joy

ᚹ

The glyph Wunjo represents your clan's flag. It is a symbol of restoration of a victory in battle over enemies, triumph over an adversarial person or situation. Of joy in spirit, security of person and place, safety, celebration and belonging. It portends harmony, prosperity and spiritual rewards.

Merkstave – When Wunjo lands inverted, conversely, it points towards deep sorrow, alienation of affection from someone or somethings. You know, loss.

HEIMDALLR'S AETT

In Norse mythology, Heimdallr was the watchman of the Gods.

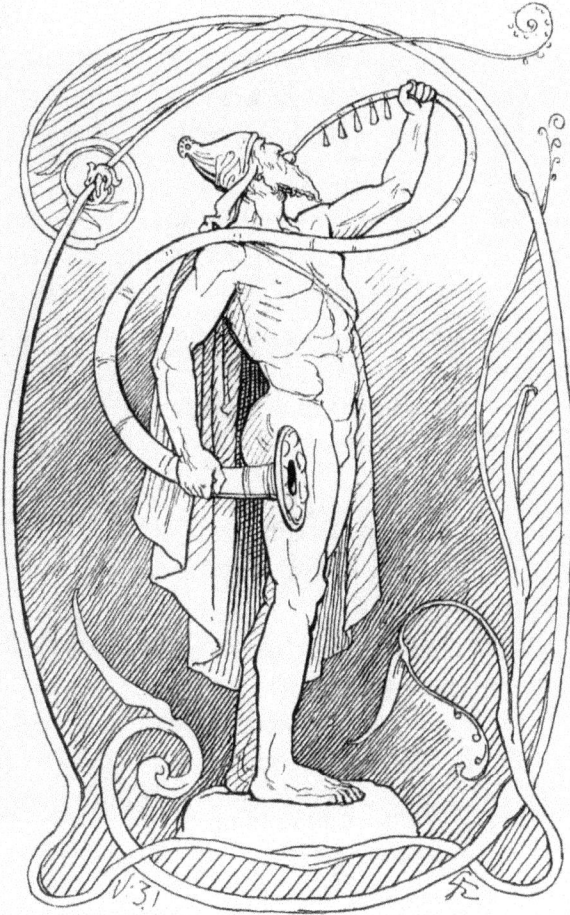

The Norse god Heimdallr with Gjallarhorn. Artwork
by Lorenz Frølich (1820-1908) Public Domain

Hagalaz – Hail

ᚺ

Hagalaz, the Awakener, represents a hail storm, a destructive force. Drawn as a rune, it relates to sudden, cataclysmic, unavoidable change imposed on our worldly dominion. Expect disruption of plans, with this great awakening. Note the actual form of awakening could be like coming to consciousness after a long sleep. Or, more dramatically, a ripping away of the fabric that once was your reality, your security, your beliefs.

Merkstave - Hagalaz has no inverted meaning.

Nauthiz – Needs

ᚾ

Nauthiz represents one's needs. An introspective rune, drawing one suggests asking the question of a deep inner reflection. Ask oneself what is needed in order to feel on a solid emotional footing? What's need to be fulfilled? Do you balance work, and play? It can warn of delays, restriction, and the need for patience.

Merkstave - Nauthiz inverted points to depression lowering of physical or mental vitality, scarcity, and misfortune

Isa - Ice

Isa represents ice. When drawn, it highlights the need to pause, to wait for the spring thaw. With a ship stuck in arctic ice, progress is unlikely, if not downright impossible. Like the fallow period preceding a rebirth, one feels powerless to do anything other than to submit to frustration or or psychological blocks. Surrender, Be patient, Sometimes enduring a break is needed to gain perspective.

Merkstave - Isa does not have any inverted meaning.

Jera – Harvest

Jera, the Rune of profitable outcome, represents a harvest and applies to an endeavor to which you are pursuing. That said, do not naively expect a quick resolution. Remain positive but know that a full cycle of mother Earth's time will pass before the reaping of the plentiful harvest or deliverance.

Merkstave - Jera does not have an inverted meaning.

Eihwaz - Yew

In Norse mythology, the Yew tree, Yggradisil, The Tree Of Life, relates to the cycle of life. Drawing an upright Eihwaz announces a time of waiting, counseling on the wisdom of patience, of not rushing pell mell towards a desired outcome. Wisdom, perseverance is appropriate along with the ability to foresee consequences before acting.

Merkstave - Reversed, Eihwaz might mean destruction and confusion.

Perthro - Destiny

Perthro represents fate, the casting of dice, or chance. Drawing it suggests life may be down to chance, to the wheel of fortune. One's destiny can either go well or not well. An element of the unknown, it represents secret matters, obscured meanings, prophecy and change.

Merkstave – Perthro, cast in the inverted position, indicates a slowdown, or the loss of hope or faith.

Algiz - Elk

Algiz, the elk, the rune of protection, represents defense and clairvoyance. Some sage students of the rune assert that Algiz is a mirror for a Spiritual Warrior while in transition, walking the path of knowledge, of self improvement. One whose only battle is with the self. Drawing this rune means an awakening and strong clairvoyant forces. It is said to act as a raised shield guarding against evil forces.

Merkstave – Algiz, when inverted, signifies lurking danger.

Sowilo - Sun

Sowilo shines like the sun. Drawing this glyph foretells the imminent arrival of of the lush abundance of goods, of happiness and good fortune. Sowilo gives cause for celebration of aspirations achieved, for the enjoyment of good mental and physical health.

Merkstave – Drawing Sowilo – is all good and does not have an inverted meaning.

Týr's Aett]
Norse Sky God Týr represents war and justice.

The Norse god Týr, identified with Mars. From a 18th century Icelandic manuscript reposing in the care of the Icelandic National Library.

Tiwaz – Victory

↑

Tiwaz is symbolic of the warrior's arrowhead and of the deity Tyr, legendary god of justice and law. When drawn, shows you up to be eminently capable of spearheading through obstacles and possessing strong leadership traits, as in command presence and rationality. It portends victory and A confidence in your innate strength with a willingness to self-sacrifice.

Merkstave – Tiwaz, when inverted, might suggest blocked creativity, over-analysis, mental paralysis, imbalance and a lack of passion or desire.

Berkana – Birch

ᛒ

Berkana, the glyph for birth, represents the ancient Birch Goddess. Accordingly, she relates directly to the concepts of fertility and creation. Not limited to an actual birth event, Berkana applies to projects, partnerships and rebirth. On the more personal level, she represents mental and physical growth, regenerative power and liberation of spirit.

Merkstave – Berkana, when inverted, points her accusing finger at anxiety, family discord, carelessness and loss of control.

Ehwaz – Horse

ᛗ

Ehwaz, the horse, is the rune of movement, of transition. When drawn it represents moving forward, a change for the better, albeit by means of gradual, steady progress. It also shows teamwork, trust and loyalty.

Ehwaz drawn inverted shows a restlessness of nature, strong craving , mistrust or disharmony.

Mannaz – Man

ᛗ

Mannaz represents mankind and humanity, one's personal identity, the sense of self and relationships with others, either enjoyed or endured. Drawing this rune is positive, pointing to good social order, a sense of community and cooperation.

Merkstave – Mannaz in the inverted position indicates self-delusion, manipulation and isolation.

Laguz – Lake

Laguz represents the element of water and is intrinsically linked to emotions, dreams and intuition. It represents healing of the body or the soul. It is the power of renewal, heightened imagination and psychic abilities. It relates to dark secrets, mysteries, the unknown and the underworld.

Merkstave - Inverted, Laguz points to fear, faulty judgment, lack of creativity, denial and avoidance.

Ingwaz – Fertility

Ingwaz is the rune of fertility, representing the Earth God Ing, pointing to male fertility, common virtues, common sense, well-being, strength, family, rest, and loose ends being tied up.

Merkstave - Ingwaz does not have an inverted meaning.

Othala – Heritage

Othala is the Rune of acquisition and benefits, and as such it speaks to birthright and spiritual heritage. Counter intuitively, it may relate to something you value that you will be called up to abandon, such as an attachment to your position in society, as beloved friend, the work you do or perhaps a long-established belief system.

Merkstave – Othala inverted warns of bad Karma and prejudice.

Dagaz – Dawn

Dagaz represents dawn. Illuminating the coming of age and the ending of a previous cycle of life. The twilight points towards an awakening, new beginnings, a breakthrough, a more fully awareness consciousness. Drawing this rune alludes to the transforming power of change and signals how the present is a good time to embark upon a fresh enterprise. In sum, Dagaz is a positive symbol of hope, certitude and security.

Merkstave – Inverted position, the Dagaz rune stone, has no meaning.

How to Use This Journal

- Clear your mind..
- Take a deep breath and exhale.
- Relax.
- Let go of all your worries and cares.
- Imagine them leaving your body along with the breath you let out.
- Purposefully cast the runes in whatever pattern you have chosen.
- Pose a question. Write it down in the space provided.
- Draw a single rune.
- Each time you draw a rune for interpretation, dutifully record which one it was in the table provided. Notice how each individual rune resides neatly in its own little box.
- More particularly, when a rune is drawn upright, scribe a tick mark above that particular rune.
- Conversely, when a rune is drawn inverted, make a tick mark below that particular rune.
- Pause for a moment between drawing runes to think about the rune drawn before picking the next one out of the pile.
- Record your interpretation.
- Take action in your life.

Date: __/ __/ _____

When drawn upright, place a checkmark above each rune drawn.
When drawn inverted, simply mark below the rune.

Algiz - Elk	Ansuz - Message	Berkana – Birch	Dagaz- Dawn	Ehwaz - Horse	Eihwaz - Yew
Fehu – Cattle, wealth	Gebo - Gift	Hagalaz – Hail	Ingwaz – Fertility	Isa - Ice	Jera - Harvest
Kenaz - torch	Laguz - Lake	Mannaz – Man	Nauthiz - Needs	Othala - Heritage	Pertho - Destiny
Raidho -Journey	Sowilo – Sun	Thurisaz - Mallet/giant	Tiwaz- Victory	Uruz - Ox	Wunjo – Joy

Question Asked:

Interpretation of the Reading

Date: __/ __/ _____

When drawn upright, place a checkmark above each rune drawn.
When drawn inverted, simply mark below the rune.

ᛉ	ᚠ	ᛒ	ᛞ	ᛗ	ᛇ
Algiz - Elk	Ansuz - Message	Berkana – Birch	Dagaz- Dawn	Ehwaz - Horse	Eihwaz - Yew
ᚡ	ᚷ	ᚺ	◇	ᛁ	ᚴ
Fehu – Cattle, wealth	Gebo - Gift	Hagalaz – Hail	Ingwaz – Fertility	Isa - Ice	Jera - Harvest
ᚲ	ᛚ	ᛘ	ᚾ	ᛟ	ᛈ
Kenaz - torch	Laguz - Lake	Mannaz – Man	Nauthiz - Needs	Othala - Heritage	Pertho - Destiny
ᚱ	ᛋ	ᚦ	ᛏ	ᚢ	ᚹ
Raidho -Journey	Sowilo – Sun	Thurisaz Mallet/gia nt	Tiwaz- Victory	Uruz - Ox	Wunjo – Joy

Question Asked:

Interpretation of the Reading

When drawn upright, place a checkmark above each rune drawn.
When drawn inverted, simply mark below the rune.

Algiz - Elk	Ansuz - Message	Berkana – Birch	Dagaz- Dawn	Ehwaz - Horse	Eihwaz - Yew
Fehu – Cattle, wealth	Gebo - Gift	Hagalaz – Hail	Ingwaz – Fertility	Isa - Ice	Jera - Harvest
Kenaz - torch	Laguz - Lake	Mannaz – Man	Nauthiz - Needs	Othala - Heritage	Pertho - Destiny
Raidho -Journey	Sowilo – Sun	Thurisaz Mallet/gia nt	Tiwaz- Victory	Uruz - Ox	Wunjo – Joy

Question Asked:

Interpretation of the Reading

When drawn upright, place a checkmark above each rune drawn.
When drawn inverted, simply mark below the rune.

Algiz - Elk	Ansuz - Message	Berkana – Birch	Dagaz- Dawn	Ehwaz - Horse	Eihwaz - Yew
Fehu – Cattle, wealth	Gebo - Gift	Hagalaz – Hail	Ingwaz – Fertility	Isa - Ice	Jera - Harvest
Kenaz - torch	Laguz - Lake	Mannaz – Man	Nauthiz - Needs	Othala - Heritage	Pertho - Destiny
Raidho -Journey	Sowilo – Sun	Thurisaz Mallet/gia nt	Tiwaz- Victory	Uruz - Ox	Wunjo – Joy

Question Asked:

Interpretation of the Reading

Date: __/ __/ _____

When drawn upright, place a checkmark above each rune drawn.
When drawn inverted, simply mark below the rune.

Algiz - Elk	Ansuz - Message	Berkana – Birch	Dagaz- Dawn	Ehwaz - Horse	Eihwaz - Yew
Fehu – Cattle, wealth	Gebo - Gift	Hagalaz – Hail	Ingwaz – Fertility	Isa - Ice	Jera - Harvest
Kenaz - torch	Laguz - Lake	Mannaz – Man	Nauthiz - Needs	Othala - Heritage	Pertho - Destiny
Raidho -Journey	Sowilo – Sun	Thurisaz Mallet/giant	Tiwaz- Victory	Uruz - Ox	Wunjo – Joy

Question Asked:

Interpretation of the Reading

When drawn upright, place a checkmark above each rune drawn.
When drawn inverted, simply mark below the rune.

Algiz - Elk	Ansuz - Message	Berkana – Birch	Dagaz- Dawn	Ehwaz - Horse	Eihwaz - Yew
Fehu – Cattle, wealth	Gebo - Gift	Hagalaz – Hail	Ingwaz – Fertility	Isa - Ice	Jera - Harvest
Kenaz - torch	Laguz - Lake	Mannaz – Man	Nauthiz - Needs	Othala - Heritage	Pertho - Destiny
Raidho -Journey	Sowilo – Sun	Thurisaz Mallet/giant	Tiwaz- Victory	Uruz - Ox	Wunjo – Joy

Question Asked:

Interpretation of the Reading

When drawn upright, place a checkmark above each rune drawn.
When drawn inverted, simply mark below the rune.

Algiz - Elk	Ansuz - Message	Berkana – Birch	Dagaz- Dawn	Ehwaz - Horse	Eihwaz - Yew
Fehu – Cattle, wealth	Gebo - Gift	Hagalaz – Hail	Ingwaz – Fertility	Isa - Ice	Jera - Harvest
Kenaz - torch	Laguz - Lake	Mannaz – Man	Nauthiz - Needs	Othala - Heritage	Pertho - Destiny
Raidho -Journey	Sowilo – Sun	Thurisaz Mallet/gia nt	Tiwaz- Victory	Uruz - Ox	Wunjo – Joy

Question Asked:

Interpretation of the Reading

Date: __/__/_____

When drawn upright, place a checkmark above each rune drawn.
When drawn inverted, simply mark below the rune.

ᛦ	ᚠ	ᛒ	ᛝ	ᛗ	ᛇ
Algiz - Elk	Ansuz - Message	Berkana – Birch	Dagaz- Dawn	Ehwaz - Horse	Eihwaz - Yew
ᚡ	ᚷ	ᚺ	◊	ᛁ	ᛋ
Fehu – Cattle, wealth	Gebo - Gift	Hagalaz – Hail	Ingwaz – Fertility	Isa - Ice	Jera - Harvest
ᚲ	ᛚ	ᛉ	ᛏ	ᛟ	ᛈ
Kenaz - torch	Laguz - Lake	Mannaz – Man	Nauthiz - Needs	Othala - Heritage	Pertho - Destiny
ᚱ	ᛋ	ᚦ	ᛏ	ᚢ	ᚹ
Raidho -Journey	Sowilo – Sun	Thurisaz Mallet/giant	Tiwaz- Victory	Uruz - Ox	Wunjo – Joy

Question Asked:

Interpretation of the Reading

Date: __/ __/ _____

When drawn upright, place a checkmark above each rune drawn.
When drawn inverted, simply mark below the rune.

ᛉ	ᚠ	ᛒ	ᛞ	ᛗ	ᛇ
Algiz - Elk	Ansuz - Message	Berkana – Birch	Dagaz- Dawn	Ehwaz - Horse	Eihwaz - Yew
ᚡ	ᚷ	ᚺ	◊	ᛁ	ᛃ
Fehu – Cattle, wealth	Gebo - Gift	Hagalaz – Hail	Ingwaz – Fertility	Isa - Ice	Jera - Harvest
ᚲ	ᛚ	ᛗ	ᚾ	ᛜ	ᛈ
Kenaz - torch	Laguz - Lake	Mannaz – Man	Nauthiz - Needs	Othala - Heritage	Pertho - Destiny
ᚱ	ᛋ	ᚦ	ᛏ	ᚢ	ᚹ
Raidho -Journey	Sowilo – Sun	Thurisaz Mallet/giant	Tiwaz- Victory	Uruz - Ox	Wunjo – Joy

Question Asked:

Interpretation of the Reading

When drawn upright, place a checkmark above each rune drawn.
When drawn inverted, simply mark below the rune.

Algiz - Elk	Ansuz - Message	Berkana – Birch	Dagaz- Dawn	Ehwaz - Horse	Eihwaz - Yew
Fehu – Cattle, wealth	Gebo - Gift	Hagalaz – Hail	Ingwaz – Fertility	Isa - Ice	Jera - Harvest
Kenaz - torch	Laguz - Lake	Mannaz – Man	Nauthiz - Needs	Othala - Heritage	Pertho - Destiny
Raidho -Journey	Sowilo – Sun	Thurisaz Mallet/gia nt	Tiwaz- Victory	Uruz - Ox	Wunjo – Joy

Question Asked:

Interpretation of the Reading

When drawn upright, place a checkmark above each rune drawn.
When drawn inverted, simply mark below the rune.

Algiz - Elk	Ansuz - Message	Berkana – Birch	Dagaz- Dawn	Ehwaz - Horse	Eihwaz - Yew
Fehu – Cattle, wealth	Gebo - Gift	Hagalaz – Hail	Ingwaz – Fertility	Isa - Ice	Jera - Harvest
Kenaz - torch	Laguz - Lake	Mannaz – Man	Nauthiz - Needs	Othala - Heritage	Pertho - Destiny
Raidho -Journey	Sowilo – Sun	Thurisaz Mallet/giant	Tiwaz- Victory	Uruz - Ox	Wunjo – Joy

Question Asked:

Interpretation of the Reading

When drawn upright, place a checkmark above each rune drawn.
When drawn inverted, simply mark below the rune.

ᛉ Algiz - Elk	ᚠ Ansuz - Message	ᛒ Berkana – Birch	ᛞ Dagaz- Dawn	ᛗ Ehwaz - Horse	ᛇ Eihwaz - Yew
ᚠ Fehu – Cattle, wealth	ᚷ Gebo - Gift	ᚺ Hagalaz – Hail	ᛜ Ingwaz – Fertility	ᛁ Isa - Ice	ᛃ Jera - Harvest
ᚲ Kenaz - torch	ᛚ Laguz - Lake	ᛗ Mannaz – Man	ᛏ Nauthiz - Needs	ᛟ Othala - Heritage	ᛈ Pertho - Destiny
ᚱ Raidho -Journey	ᛋ Sowilo – Sun	ᚦ Thurisaz Mallet/giant	ᛏ Tiwaz- Victory	ᚢ Uruz - Ox	ᚹ Wunjo – Joy

Question Asked:

Interpretation of the Reading

Date: __/__/_____

When drawn upright, place a checkmark above each rune drawn.
When drawn inverted, simply mark below the rune.

ᛉ Algiz - Elk	ᚠ Ansuz - Message	ᛒ Berkana – Birch	ᛞ Dagaz- Dawn	ᛖ Ehwaz - Horse	ᛇ Eihwaz - Yew
ᚡ Fehu – Cattle, wealth	ᚷ Gebo - Gift	ᚺ Hagalaz – Hail	ᛜ Ingwaz – Fertility	ᛁ Isa - Ice	ᛃ Jera - Harvest
ᚲ Kenaz - torch	ᛚ Laguz - Lake	ᛗ Mannaz – Man	ᚾ Nauthiz - Needs	ᛟ Othala - Heritage	ᛈ Pertho - Destiny
ᚱ Raidho -Journey	ᛊ Sowilo – Sun	ᚦ Thurisaz Mallet/giant	ᛏ Tiwaz- Victory	ᚢ Uruz - Ox	ᚹ Wunjo – Joy

Question Asked:

Interpretation of the Reading

When drawn upright, place a checkmark above each rune drawn.
When drawn inverted, simply mark below the rune.

Algiz - Elk	Ansuz - Message	Berkana – Birch	Dagaz- Dawn	Ehwaz - Horse	Eihwaz - Yew
Fehu – Cattle, wealth	Gebo - Gift	Hagalaz – Hail	Ingwaz – Fertility	Isa - Ice	Jera - Harvest
Kenaz - torch	Laguz - Lake	Mannaz – Man	Nauthiz - Needs	Othala - Heritage	Pertho - Destiny
Raidho -Journey	Sowilo – Sun	Thurisaz Mallet/gia nt	Tiwaz- Victory	Uruz - Ox	Wunjo – Joy

Question Asked:

Interpretation of the Reading

When drawn upright, place a checkmark above each rune drawn.
When drawn inverted, simply mark below the rune.

Algiz - Elk	Ansuz - Message	Berkana – Birch	Dagaz- Dawn	Ehwaz - Horse	Eihwaz - Yew
Fehu – Cattle, wealth	Gebo - Gift	Hagalaz – Hail	Ingwaz – Fertility	Isa - Ice	Jera - Harvest
Kenaz - torch	Laguz - Lake	Mannaz – Man	Nauthiz - Needs	Othala - Heritage	Pertho - Destiny
Raidho -Journey	Sowilo – Sun	Thurisaz Mallet/gia nt	Tiwaz- Victory	Uruz - Ox	Wunjo – Joy

Question Asked:

Interpretation of the Reading

When drawn upright, place a checkmark above each rune drawn.
When drawn inverted, simply mark below the rune.

Algiz - Elk	Ansuz - Message	Berkana – Birch	Dagaz- Dawn	Ehwaz - Horse	Eihwaz - Yew
Fehu – Cattle, wealth	Gebo - Gift	Hagalaz – Hail	Ingwaz – Fertility	Isa - Ice	Jera - Harvest
Kenaz - torch	Laguz - Lake	Mannaz – Man	Nauthiz - Needs	Othala - Heritage	Pertho - Destiny
Raidho -Journey	Sowilo – Sun	Thurisaz Mallet/giant	Tiwaz- Victory	Uruz - Ox	Wunjo – Joy

Question Asked:

Interpretation of the Reading

Date: __/ __/ _____

When drawn upright, place a checkmark above each rune drawn.
When drawn inverted, simply mark below the rune.

ᛉ	ᚠ	ᛒ	ᛞ	ᛗ	ᛇ
Algiz - Elk	Ansuz - Message	Berkana – Birch	Dagaz- Dawn	Ehwaz - Horse	Eihwaz - Yew
ᚠ	ᚷ	ᚺ	◇	ᛁ	ᛃ
Fehu – Cattle, wealth	Gebo - Gift	Hagalaz – Hail	Ingwaz – Fertility	Isa - Ice	Jera - Harvest
ᚲ	ᛚ	ᛗ	ᛏ	ᛟ	ᛈ
Kenaz - torch	Laguz - Lake	Mannaz – Man	Nauthiz - Needs	Othala - Heritage	Pertho - Destiny
ᚱ	ᛋ	ᚦ	ᛏ	ᚢ	ᚹ
Raidho -Journey	Sowilo – Sun	Thurisaz Mallet/gia nt	Tiwaz- Victory	Uruz - Ox	Wunjo – Joy

Question Asked:

Interpretation of the Reading

When drawn upright, place a checkmark above each rune drawn.
When drawn inverted, simply mark below the rune.

Algiz - Elk	Ansuz - Message	Berkana – Birch	Dagaz- Dawn	Ehwaz - Horse	Eihwaz - Yew
Fehu – Cattle, wealth	Gebo - Gift	Hagalaz – Hail	Ingwaz – Fertility	Isa - Ice	Jera - Harvest
Kenaz - torch	Laguz - Lake	Mannaz – Man	Nauthiz - Needs	Othala - Heritage	Pertho - Destiny
Raidho -Journey	Sowilo – Sun	Thurisaz Mallet/giant	Tiwaz- Victory	Uruz - Ox	Wunjo – Joy

Question Asked:

Interpretation of the Reading

Date: __/ __/ _____

When drawn upright, place a checkmark above each rune drawn.
When drawn inverted, simply mark below the rune.

Algiz - Elk	Ansuz - Message	Berkana – Birch	Dagaz- Dawn	Ehwaz - Horse	Eihwaz - Yew
Fehu – Cattle, wealth	Gebo - Gift	Hagalaz – Hail	Ingwaz – Fertility	Isa - Ice	Jera - Harvest
Kenaz - torch	Laguz - Lake	Mannaz – Man	Nauthiz - Needs	Othala - Heritage	Pertho - Destiny
Raidho -Journey	Sowilo – Sun	Thurisaz Mallet/giant	Tiwaz- Victory	Uruz - Ox	Wunjo – Joy

Question Asked:

Interpretation of the Reading

Date: __/ __/ _____

When drawn upright, place a checkmark above each rune drawn.
When drawn inverted, simply mark below the rune.

Algiz - Elk	Ansuz - Message	Berkana – Birch	Dagaz- Dawn	Ehwaz - Horse	Eihwaz - Yew
Fehu – Cattle, wealth	Gebo - Gift	Hagalaz – Hail	Ingwaz – Fertility	Isa - Ice	Jera - Harvest
Kenaz - torch	Laguz - Lake	Mannaz – Man	Nauthiz - Needs	Othala - Heritage	Pertho - Destiny
Raidho -Journey	Sowilo – Sun	Thurisaz Mallet/gia nt	Tiwaz- Victory	Uruz - Ox	Wunjo – Joy

Question Asked:

Interpretation of the Reading

Date: __/__/_____

When drawn upright, place a checkmark above each rune drawn.
When drawn inverted, simply mark below the rune.

ᛉ	ᚠ	ᛒ	ᛞ	ᛗ	ᛇ
Algiz - Elk	Ansuz - Message	Berkana – Birch	Dagaz- Dawn	Ehwaz - Horse	Eihwaz - Yew
ᚡ	ᚷ	ᚺ	◊	ᛁ	ᛃ
Fehu – Cattle, wealth	Gebo - Gift	Hagalaz – Hail	Ingwaz – Fertility	Isa - Ice	Jera - Harvest
ᚲ	ᛚ	ᛗ	ᛏ	ᛟ	ᛈ
Kenaz - torch	Laguz - Lake	Mannaz – Man	Nauthiz - Needs	Othala - Heritage	Pertho - Destiny
ᚱ	ᛋ	ᚦ	ᛏ	ᚢ	ᚹ
Raidho -Journey	Sowilo – Sun	Thurisaz Mallet/giant	Tiwaz- Victory	Uruz - Ox	Wunjo – Joy

Question Asked:

Interpretation of the Reading

Date: __/ __/ _____

When drawn upright, place a checkmark above each rune drawn.
When drawn inverted, simply mark below the rune.

Algiz - Elk	Ansuz - Message	Berkana – Birch	Dagaz- Dawn	Ehwaz - Horse	Eihwaz - Yew
Fehu – Cattle, wealth	Gebo - Gift	Hagalaz – Hail	Ingwaz – Fertility	Isa - Ice	Jera - Harvest
Kenaz - torch	Laguz - Lake	Mannaz – Man	Nauthiz - Needs	Othala - Heritage	Pertho - Destiny
Raidho -Journey	Sowilo – Sun	Thurisaz Mallet/giant	Tiwaz- Victory	Uruz - Ox	Wunjo – Joy

Question Asked:

Interpretation of the Reading

When drawn upright, place a checkmark above each rune drawn.
When drawn inverted, simply mark below the rune.

ᛉ Algiz - Elk	ᚠ Ansuz - Message	ᛒ Berkana – Birch	ᛞ Dagaz- Dawn	ᛗ Ehwaz - Horse	ᛃ Eihwaz - Yew
ᚡ Fehu – Cattle, wealth	ᚷ Gebo - Gift	ᚺ Hagalaz – Hail	◇ Ingwaz – Fertility	ᛁ Isa - Ice	ᛋ Jera - Harvest
ᚲ Kenaz - torch	ᛚ Laguz - Lake	ᛗ Mannaz – Man	ᛏ Nauthiz - Needs	ᛜ Othala - Heritage	ᛈ Pertho - Destiny
ᚱ Raidho -Journey	ᛋ Sowilo – Sun	ᚦ Thurisaz Mallet/giant	ᛏ Tiwaz- Victory	ᚢ Uruz - Ox	ᚹ Wunjo – Joy

Question Asked:

Interpretation of the Reading

67

Date: __/__/_____

When drawn upright, place a checkmark above each rune drawn.
When drawn inverted, simply mark below the rune.

ᛉ Algiz - Elk	ᚨ Ansuz - Message	ᛒ Berkana – Birch	ᛞ Dagaz- Dawn	ᛗ Ehwaz - Horse	ᛃ Eihwaz - Yew
ᚠ Fehu – Cattle, wealth	ᚷ Gebo - Gift	ᚺ Hagalaz – Hail	◇ Ingwaz – Fertility	ᛁ Isa - Ice	ᛋ Jera - Harvest
ᚲ Kenaz - torch	ᛚ Laguz - Lake	ᛗ Mannaz – Man	ᛏ Nauthiz - Needs	ᛟ Othala - Heritage	ᛈ Pertho - Destiny
ᚱ Raidho -Journey	ᛋ Sowilo – Sun	ᚦ Thurisaz Mallet/giant	↑ Tiwaz- Victory	ᚢ Uruz - Ox	ᚹ Wunjo – Joy

Question Asked:

Interpretation of the Reading

When drawn upright, place a checkmark above each rune drawn.
When drawn inverted, simply mark below the rune.

Algiz - Elk	Ansuz - Message	Berkana – Birch	Dagaz- Dawn	Ehwaz - Horse	Eihwaz - Yew
Fehu – Cattle, wealth	Gebo - Gift	Hagalaz – Hail	Ingwaz – Fertility	Isa - Ice	Jera - Harvest
Kenaz - torch	Laguz - Lake	Mannaz – Man	Nauthiz - Needs	Othala - Heritage	Pertho - Destiny
Raidho -Journey	Sowilo – Sun	Thurisaz Mallet/gia nt	Tiwaz- Victory	Uruz - Ox	Wunjo – Joy

Question Asked:

Interpretation of the Reading

Date: __/ __/ _____

When drawn upright, place a checkmark above each rune drawn.
When drawn inverted, simply mark below the rune.

Algiz - Elk	Ansuz - Message	Berkana – Birch	Dagaz- Dawn	Ehwaz - Horse	Eihwaz - Yew
Fehu – Cattle, wealth	Gebo - Gift	Hagalaz – Hail	Ingwaz – Fertility	Isa - Ice	Jera - Harvest
Kenaz - torch	Laguz - Lake	Mannaz – Man	Nauthiz - Needs	Othala - Heritage	Pertho - Destiny
Raidho -Journey	Sowilo – Sun	Thurisaz Mallet/giant	Tiwaz- Victory	Uruz - Ox	Wunjo – Joy

Question Asked:

Interpretation of the Reading

Date: __/ __/ _____

When drawn upright, place a checkmark above each rune drawn.
When drawn inverted, simply mark below the rune.

ᛉ	ᚠ	ᛒ	ᛞ	ᛗ	ᛇ
Algiz - Elk	Ansuz - Message	Berkana – Birch	Dagaz- Dawn	Ehwaz - Horse	Eihwaz - Yew
ᚡ	ᚷ	ᚺ	◇	|	ᛋ
Fehu – Cattle, wealth	Gebo - Gift	Hagalaz – Hail	Ingwaz – Fertility	Isa - Ice	Jera - Harvest
ᚲ	ᛚ	ᛗ	ᛏ	ᛟ	ᛈ
Kenaz - torch	Laguz - Lake	Mannaz – Man	Nauthiz - Needs	Othala - Heritage	Pertho - Destiny
ᚱ	ᛋ	ᚦ	ᛏ	ᚢ	ᚹ
Raidho -Journey	Sowilo – Sun	Thurisaz - Mallet/giant	Tiwaz- Victory	Uruz - Ox	Wunjo – Joy

Question Asked:

Interpretation of the Reading

When drawn upright, place a checkmark above each rune drawn.
When drawn inverted, simply mark below the rune.

ᛉ	ᚠ	ᛒ	ᛞ	ᛖ	ᛇ
Algiz - Elk	Ansuz - Message	Berkana – Birch	Dagaz- Dawn	Ehwaz - Horse	Eihwaz - Yew
ᚠ	ᚷ	ᚺ	◇	ᛁ	ᛃ
Fehu – Cattle, wealth	Gebo - Gift	Hagalaz – Hail	Ingwaz – Fertility	Isa - Ice	Jera - Harvest
ᚲ	ᛚ	ᛗ	ᛏ	ᛟ	ᛈ
Kenaz - torch	Laguz - Lake	Mannaz – Man	Nauthiz - Needs	Othala - Heritage	Pertho - Destiny
ᚱ	ᛋ	ᚦ	ᛏ	ᚢ	ᚹ
Raidho -Journey	Sowilo – Sun	Thurisaz - Mallet/gia nt	Tiwaz- Victory	Uruz - Ox	Wunjo – Joy

Question Asked:

Interpretation of the Reading

When drawn upright, place a checkmark above each rune drawn.
When drawn inverted, simply mark below the rune.

Algiz - Elk	Ansuz - Message	Berkana – Birch	Dagaz- Dawn	Ehwaz - Horse	Eihwaz - Yew
Fehu – Cattle, wealth	Gebo - Gift	Hagalaz – Hail	Ingwaz – Fertility	Isa - Ice	Jera - Harvest
Kenaz - torch	Laguz - Lake	Mannaz – Man	Nauthiz - Needs	Othala - Heritage	Pertho - Destiny
Raidho -Journey	Sowilo – Sun	Thurisaz Mallet/giant	Tiwaz- Victory	Uruz - Ox	Wunjo – Joy

Question Asked:

Interpretation of the Reading

When drawn upright, place a checkmark above each rune drawn.
When drawn inverted, simply mark below the rune.

Algiz - Elk	Ansuz - Message	Berkana – Birch	Dagaz- Dawn	Ehwaz - Horse	Eihwaz - Yew
Fehu – Cattle, wealth	Gebo - Gift	Hagalaz – Hail	Ingwaz – Fertility	Isa - Ice	Jera - Harvest
Kenaz - torch	Laguz - Lake	Mannaz – Man	Nauthiz - Needs	Othala - Heritage	Pertho - Destiny
Raidho -Journey	Sowilo – Sun	Thurisaz Mallet/giant	Tiwaz- Victory	Uruz - Ox	Wunjo – Joy

Question Asked:

Interpretation of the Reading

When drawn upright, place a checkmark above each rune drawn.
When drawn inverted, simply mark below the rune.

Algiz - Elk	Ansuz - Message	Berkana – Birch	Dagaz- Dawn	Ehwaz - Horse	Eihwaz - Yew
Fehu – Cattle, wealth	Gebo - Gift	Hagalaz – Hail	Ingwaz – Fertility	Isa - Ice	Jera - Harvest
Kenaz - torch	Laguz - Lake	Mannaz – Man	Nauthiz - Needs	Othala - Heritage	Pertho - Destiny
Raidho -Journey	Sowilo – Sun	Thurisaz Mallet/giant	Tiwaz- Victory	Uruz - Ox	Wunjo – Joy

Question Asked:

Interpretation of the Reading

Date: __/ __/ _____

When drawn upright, place a checkmark above each rune drawn.
When drawn inverted, simply mark below the rune.

ᛉ	ᚠ	ᛒ	ᛞ	ᛗ	ᛇ
Algiz - Elk	Ansuz - Message	Berkana – Birch	Dagaz- Dawn	Ehwaz - Horse	Eihwaz - Yew
ᚩ	ᚷ	ᚺ	◇	⎮	ᛃ
Fehu – Cattle, wealth	Gebo - Gift	Hagalaz – Hail	Ingwaz – Fertility	Isa - Ice	Jera - Harvest
ᚲ	ᛚ	ᛗ	ᛏ	ᛟ	ᛈ
Kenaz - torch	Laguz - Lake	Mannaz – Man	Nauthiz - Needs	Othala - Heritage	Pertho - Destiny
ᚱ	ᛋ	ᚦ	ᛏ	ᚢ	ᚹ
Raidho -Journey	Sowilo – Sun	Thurisaz Mallet/gia nt	Tiwaz- Victory	Uruz - Ox	Wunjo – Joy

Question Asked:

Interpretation of the Reading

Date: __/ __/ _____

When drawn upright, place a checkmark above each rune drawn.
When drawn inverted, simply mark below the rune.

Algiz - Elk	Ansuz - Message	Berkana – Birch	Dagaz- Dawn	Ehwaz - Horse	Eihwaz - Yew
Fehu – Cattle, wealth	Gebo - Gift	Hagalaz – Hail	Ingwaz – Fertility	Isa - Ice	Jera - Harvest
Kenaz - torch	Laguz - Lake	Mannaz – Man	Nauthiz - Needs	Othala - Heritage	Pertho - Destiny
Raidho -Journey	Sowilo – Sun	Thurisaz Mallet/giant	Tiwaz- Victory	Uruz - Ox	Wunjo – Joy

Question Asked:

Interpretation of the Reading

Date: __/ __/ _____

When drawn upright, place a checkmark above each rune drawn.
When drawn inverted, simply mark below the rune.

ᛉ Algiz - Elk	ᚠ Ansuz - Message	ᛒ Berkana – Birch	ᛞ Dagaz- Dawn	ᛗ Ehwaz - Horse	ᛇ Eihwaz - Yew
ᚠ Fehu – Cattle, wealth	ᚷ Gebo - Gift	ᚺ Hagalaz – Hail	ᛜ Ingwaz – Fertility	ᛁ Isa - Ice	ᛃ Jera - Harvest
ᚲ Kenaz - torch	ᛚ Laguz - Lake	ᛗ Mannaz – Man	ᛏ Nauthiz - Needs	ᛟ Othala - Heritage	ᛈ Pertho - Destiny
ᚱ Raidho -Journey	ᛋ Sowilo – Sun	ᚦ Thurisaz Mallet/giant	ᛏ Tiwaz- Victory	ᚢ Uruz - Ox	ᚹ Wunjo – Joy

Question Asked:

Interpretation of the Reading

Date: __/__/_____

When drawn upright, place a checkmark above each rune drawn.
When drawn inverted, simply mark below the rune.

Algiz - Elk	Ansuz - Message	Berkana – Birch	Dagaz- Dawn	Ehwaz - Horse	Eihwaz - Yew
Fehu – Cattle, wealth	Gebo - Gift	Hagalaz – Hail	Ingwaz – Fertility	Isa - Ice	Jera - Harvest
Kenaz - torch	Laguz - Lake	Mannaz – Man	Nauthiz - Needs	Othala - Heritage	Pertho - Destiny
Raidho -Journey	Sowilo – Sun	Thurisaz Mallet/giant	Tiwaz- Victory	Uruz - Ox	Wunjo – Joy

Question Asked:

Interpretation of the Reading

When drawn upright, place a checkmark above each rune drawn.
When drawn inverted, simply mark below the rune.

Algiz - Elk	Ansuz - Message	Berkana – Birch	Dagaz- Dawn	Ehwaz - Horse	Eihwaz - Yew
Fehu – Cattle, wealth	Gebo - Gift	Hagalaz – Hail	Ingwaz – Fertility	Isa - Ice	Jera - Harvest
Kenaz - torch	Laguz - Lake	Mannaz – Man	Nauthiz - Needs	Othala - Heritage	Pertho - Destiny
Raidho -Journey	Sowilo – Sun	Thurisaz Mallet/giant	Tiwaz- Victory	Uruz - Ox	Wunjo – Joy

Question Asked:

Interpretation of the Reading

When drawn upright, place a checkmark above each rune drawn.
When drawn inverted, simply mark below the rune.

Ψ	F	B	⋈	M	ʃ
Algiz - Elk	Ansuz - Message	Berkana – Birch	Dagaz- Dawn	Ehwaz - Horse	Eihwaz - Yew
Ᵽ	X	H	◇	|	⟨
Fehu – Cattle, wealth	Gebo - Gift	Hagalaz – Hail	Ingwaz – Fertility	Isa - Ice	Jera - Harvest
⟨	Γ	M	†	⊗	Ϲ
Kenaz - torch	Laguz - Lake	Mannaz – Man	Nauthiz - Needs	Othala - Heritage	Pertho - Destiny
R	S	Þ	↑	Ν	Ᵽ
Raidho -Journey	Sowilo – Sun	Thurisaz Mallet/gia nt	Tiwaz- Victory	Uruz - Ox	Wunjo – Joy

Question Asked:

Interpretation of the Reading

Date: __/__/_____

When drawn upright, place a checkmark above each rune drawn.
When drawn inverted, simply mark below the rune.

ᛉ Algiz - Elk	ᚠ Ansuz - Message	ᛒ Berkana – Birch	ᛞ Dagaz- Dawn	ᛗ Ehwaz - Horse	ᛇ Eihwaz - Yew
ᚠ Fehu – Cattle, wealth	ᚷ Gebo - Gift	ᚺ Hagalaz – Hail	ᛜ Ingwaz – Fertility	ᛁ Isa - Ice	ᛃ Jera - Harvest
ᚲ Kenaz - torch	ᛚ Laguz - Lake	ᛗ Mannaz – Man	ᚾ Nauthiz - Needs	ᛟ Othala - Heritage	ᛈ Pertho - Destiny
ᚱ Raidho -Journey	ᛋ Sowilo – Sun	ᚦ Thurisaz Mallet/giant	ᛏ Tiwaz- Victory	ᚢ Uruz - Ox	ᚹ Wunjo – Joy

Question Asked:

Interpretation of the Reading

Date: __/__/_____

When drawn upright, place a checkmark above each rune drawn.
When drawn inverted, simply mark below the rune.

Algiz - Elk	Ansuz - Message	Berkana – Birch	Dagaz- Dawn	Ehwaz - Horse	Eihwaz - Yew
Fehu – Cattle, wealth	Gebo - Gift	Hagalaz – Hail	Ingwaz – Fertility	Isa - Ice	Jera - Harvest
Kenaz - torch	Laguz - Lake	Mannaz – Man	Nauthiz - Needs	Othala - Heritage	Pertho - Destiny
Raidho -Journey	Sowilo – Sun	Thurisaz Mallet/giant	Tiwaz- Victory	Uruz - Ox	Wunjo – Joy

Question Asked:

Interpretation of the Reading

Date: __/ __/ _____

When drawn upright, place a checkmark above each rune drawn.
When drawn inverted, simply mark below the rune.

Algiz - Elk	Ansuz - Message	Berkana – Birch	Dagaz- Dawn	Ehwaz - Horse	Eihwaz - Yew
Fehu – Cattle, wealth	Gebo - Gift	Hagalaz – Hail	Ingwaz – Fertility	Isa - Ice	Jera - Harvest
Kenaz - torch	Laguz - Lake	Mannaz – Man	Nauthiz - Needs	Othala - Heritage	Pertho - Destiny
Raidho -Journey	Sowilo – Sun	Thurisaz Mallet/giant	Tiwaz- Victory	Uruz - Ox	Wunjo – Joy

Question Asked:

Interpretation of the Reading

Date: __/ __/ _____

When drawn upright, place a checkmark above each rune drawn.
When drawn inverted, simply mark below the rune.

ᛉ	ᚠ	ᛒ	ᛞ	ᛖ	ᛇ
Algiz - Elk	Ansuz - Message	Berkana – Birch	Dagaz- Dawn	Ehwaz - Horse	Eihwaz - Yew
ᚨ	ᚷ	ᚺ	◇	|	ᛃ
Fehu – Cattle, wealth	Gebo - Gift	Hagalaz – Hail	Ingwaz – Fertility	Isa - Ice	Jera - Harvest
ᚲ	ᛚ	ᛗ	ᛏ	ᛟ	ᛈ
Kenaz - torch	Laguz - Lake	Mannaz – Man	Nauthiz - Needs	Othala - Heritage	Pertho - Destiny
ᚱ	ᛊ	ᚦ	ᛏ	ᚢ	ᚹ
Raidho -Journey	Sowilo – Sun	Thurisaz Mallet/giant	Tiwaz- Victory	Uruz - Ox	Wunjo – Joy

Question Asked:

Interpretation of the Reading

Date: __/ __/ _____

When drawn upright, place a checkmark above each rune drawn.
When drawn inverted, simply mark below the rune.

Algiz - Elk	Ansuz - Message	Berkana – Birch	Dagaz- Dawn	Ehwaz - Horse	Eihwaz - Yew
Fehu – Cattle, wealth	Gebo - Gift	Hagalaz – Hail	Ingwaz – Fertility	Isa - Ice	Jera - Harvest
Kenaz - torch	Laguz - Lake	Mannaz – Man	Nauthiz - Needs	Othala - Heritage	Pertho - Destiny
Raidho -Journey	Sowilo – Sun	Thurisaz Mallet/gia nt	Tiwaz- Victory	Uruz - Ox	Wunjo – Joy

Question Asked:

Interpretation of the Reading

When drawn upright, place a checkmark above each rune drawn.
When drawn inverted, simply mark below the rune.

Algiz - Elk	Ansuz - Message	Berkana – Birch	Dagaz- Dawn	Ehwaz - Horse	Eihwaz - Yew
Fehu – Cattle, wealth	Gebo - Gift	Hagalaz – Hail	Ingwaz – Fertility	Isa - Ice	Jera - Harvest
Kenaz - torch	Laguz - Lake	Mannaz – Man	Nauthiz - Needs	Othala - Heritage	Pertho - Destiny
Raidho -Journey	Sowilo – Sun	Thurisaz Mallet/gia nt	Tiwaz- Victory	Uruz - Ox	Wunjo – Joy

Question Asked:

Interpretation of the Reading

When drawn upright, place a checkmark above each rune drawn.
When drawn inverted, simply mark below the rune.

Algiz - Elk	Ansuz - Message	Berkana – Birch	Dagaz- Dawn	Ehwaz - Horse	Eihwaz - Yew
Fehu – Cattle, wealth	Gebo - Gift	Hagalaz – Hail	Ingwaz – Fertility	Isa - Ice	Jera - Harvest
Kenaz - torch	Laguz - Lake	Mannaz – Man	Nauthiz - Needs	Othala - Heritage	Pertho - Destiny
Raidho -Journey	Sowilo – Sun	Thurisaz Mallet/giant	Tiwaz- Victory	Uruz - Ox	Wunjo – Joy

Question Asked:

Interpretation of the Reading

When drawn upright, place a checkmark above each rune drawn.
When drawn inverted, simply mark below the rune.

Algiz - Elk	Ansuz - Message	Berkana – Birch	Dagaz- Dawn	Ehwaz - Horse	Eihwaz - Yew
Fehu – Cattle, wealth	Gebo - Gift	Hagalaz – Hail	Ingwaz – Fertility	Isa - Ice	Jera - Harvest
Kenaz - torch	Laguz - Lake	Mannaz – Man	Nauthiz - Needs	Othala - Heritage	Pertho - Destiny
Raidho -Journey	Sowilo – Sun	Thurisaz Mallet/gia nt	Tiwaz- Victory	Uruz - Ox	Wunjo – Joy

Question Asked:

Interpretation of the Reading

Date: __/ __/ _____

When drawn upright, place a checkmark above each rune drawn.
When drawn inverted, simply mark below the rune.

ᛉ	ᚠ	ᛒ	ᛞ	ᛗ	ᛇ
Algiz - Elk	Ansuz - Message	Berkana – Birch	Dagaz- Dawn	Ehwaz - Horse	Eihwaz - Yew
ᚡ	ᚷ	ᚺ	ᛜ	ᛁ	ᛃ
Fehu – Cattle, wealth	Gebo - Gift	Hagalaz – Hail	Ingwaz – Fertility	Isa - Ice	Jera - Harvest
ᚲ	ᛚ	ᛗ	ᚾ	ᛟ	ᛈ
Kenaz - torch	Laguz - Lake	Mannaz – Man	Nauthiz - Needs	Othala - Heritage	Pertho - Destiny
ᚱ	ᛋ	ᚦ	ᛏ	ᚢ	ᚹ
Raidho -Journey	Sowilo – Sun	Thurisaz Mallet/giant	Tiwaz- Victory	Uruz - Ox	Wunjo – Joy

Question Asked:

Interpretation of the Reading

When drawn upright, place a checkmark above each rune drawn.
When drawn inverted, simply mark below the rune.

Algiz - Elk	Ansuz - Message	Berkana – Birch	Dagaz- Dawn	Ehwaz - Horse	Eihwaz - Yew
Fehu – Cattle, wealth	Gebo - Gift	Hagalaz – Hail	Ingwaz – Fertility	Isa - Ice	Jera - Harvest
Kenaz - torch	Laguz - Lake	Mannaz – Man	Nauthiz - Needs	Othala - Heritage	Pertho - Destiny
Raidho -Journey	Sowilo – Sun	Thurisaz Mallet/giant	Tiwaz- Victory	Uruz - Ox	Wunjo – Joy

Question Asked:

Interpretation of the Reading

When drawn upright, place a checkmark above each rune drawn.
When drawn inverted, simply mark below the rune.

Algiz - Elk	Ansuz - Message	Berkana – Birch	Dagaz- Dawn	Ehwaz - Horse	Eihwaz - Yew
Fehu – Cattle, wealth	Gebo - Gift	Hagalaz – Hail	Ingwaz – Fertility	Isa - Ice	Jera - Harvest
Kenaz - torch	Laguz - Lake	Mannaz – Man	Nauthiz - Needs	Othala - Heritage	Pertho - Destiny
Raidho -Journey	Sowilo – Sun	Thurisaz Mallet/gia nt	Tiwaz- Victory	Uruz - Ox	Wunjo – Joy

Question Asked:

Interpretation of the Reading

When drawn upright, place a checkmark above each rune drawn.
When drawn inverted, simply mark below the rune.

ᛉ Algiz - Elk	ᚠ Ansuz - Message	ᛒ Berkana – Birch	ᛞ Dagaz- Dawn	ᛖ Ehwaz - Horse	ᛇ Eihwaz - Yew
ᚠ Fehu – Cattle, wealth	ᚷ Gebo - Gift	ᚺ Hagalaz – Hail	◇ Ingwaz – Fertility	ᛁ Isa - Ice	Jera - Harvest
ᚲ Kenaz - torch	ᛚ Laguz - Lake	ᛗ Mannaz – Man	ᚾ Nauthiz - Needs	ᛟ Othala - Heritage	ᛈ Pertho - Destiny
ᚱ Raidho -Journey	ᛊ Sowilo – Sun	ᚦ Thurisaz Mallet/giant	ᛏ Tiwaz- Victory	ᚢ Uruz - Ox	ᚹ Wunjo – Joy

Question Asked:

Interpretation of the Reading

Date: __/ __/ _____

When drawn upright, place a checkmark above each rune drawn.
When drawn inverted, simply mark below the rune.

ᛉ	ᚠ	ᛒ	ᛞ	ᛖ	ᛇ
Algiz - Elk	Ansuz - Message	Berkana – Birch	Dagaz- Dawn	Ehwaz - Horse	Eihwaz - Yew
ᚡ	ᚷ	ᚺ	◇	ᛁ	ᛃ
Fehu – Cattle, wealth	Gebo - Gift	Hagalaz – Hail	Ingwaz – Fertility	Isa - Ice	Jera - Harvest
ᚲ	ᛚ	ᛗ	ᚾ	ᛟ	ᛈ
Kenaz - torch	Laguz - Lake	Mannaz – Man	Nauthiz - Needs	Othala - Heritage	Pertho - Destiny
ᚱ	ᛋ	ᚦ	ᛏ	ᚢ	ᚹ
Raidho -Journey	Sowilo – Sun	Thurisaz Mallet/giant	Tiwaz- Victory	Uruz - Ox	Wunjo – Joy

Question Asked:

Interpretation of the Reading

Date: __/ __/ _____

When drawn upright, place a checkmark above each rune drawn.
When drawn inverted, simply mark below the rune.

Algiz - Elk	Ansuz - Message	Berkana – Birch	Dagaz- Dawn	Ehwaz - Horse	Eihwaz - Yew
Fehu – Cattle, wealth	Gebo - Gift	Hagalaz – Hail	Ingwaz – Fertility	Isa - Ice	Jera - Harvest
Kenaz - torch	Laguz - Lake	Mannaz – Man	Nauthiz - Needs	Othala - Heritage	Pertho - Destiny
Raidho -Journey	Sowilo – Sun	Thurisaz Mallet/giant	Tiwaz- Victory	Uruz - Ox	Wunjo – Joy

Question Asked:

Interpretation of the Reading

Date: __/ __/ _____

When drawn upright, place a checkmark above each rune drawn.
When drawn inverted, simply mark below the rune.

Algiz - Elk	Ansuz - Message	Berkana – Birch	Dagaz- Dawn	Ehwaz - Horse	Eihwaz - Yew
Fehu – Cattle, wealth	Gebo - Gift	Hagalaz – Hail	Ingwaz – Fertility	Isa - Ice	Jera - Harvest
Kenaz - torch	Laguz - Lake	Mannaz – Man	Nauthiz - Needs	Othala - Heritage	Pertho - Destiny
Raidho -Journey	Sowilo – Sun	Thurisaz Mallet/giant	Tiwaz- Victory	Uruz - Ox	Wunjo – Joy

Question Asked:

Interpretation of the Reading

When drawn upright, place a checkmark above each rune drawn.
When drawn inverted, simply mark below the rune.

Algiz - Elk	Ansuz - Message	Berkana – Birch	Dagaz- Dawn	Ehwaz - Horse	Eihwaz - Yew
Fehu – Cattle, wealth	Gebo - Gift	Hagalaz – Hail	Ingwaz – Fertility	Isa - Ice	Jera - Harvest
Kenaz - torch	Laguz - Lake	Mannaz – Man	Nauthiz - Needs	Othala - Heritage	Pertho - Destiny
Raidho -Journey	Sowilo – Sun	Thurisaz Mallet/gia nt	Tiwaz- Victory	Uruz - Ox	Wunjo – Joy

Question Asked:

Interpretation of the Reading

Date: __/ __/ _____

When drawn upright, place a checkmark above each rune drawn.
When drawn inverted, simply mark below the rune.

ᛉ	ᚠ	ᛒ	ᛞ	ᛗ	ᛇ
Algiz - Elk	Ansuz - Message	Berkana – Birch	Dagaz- Dawn	Ehwaz - Horse	Eihwaz - Yew
ᚡ	ᚷ	ᚺ	◊	ᛁ	ᛃ
Fehu – Cattle, wealth	Gebo - Gift	Hagalaz – Hail	Ingwaz – Fertility	Isa - Ice	Jera - Harvest
ᚲ	ᛚ	ᛗ	ᛏ	ᛟ	ᛈ
Kenaz - torch	Laguz - Lake	Mannaz – Man	Nauthiz - Needs	Othala - Heritage	Pertho - Destiny
ᚱ	ᛋ	ᚦ	ᛏ	ᚢ	ᚹ
Raidho -Journey	Sowilo – Sun	Thurisaz Mallet/gia nt	Tiwaz- Victory	Uruz - Ox	Wunjo – Joy

Question Asked:

Interpretation of the Reading

When drawn upright, place a checkmark above each rune drawn.
When drawn inverted, simply mark below the rune.

ᛉ	ᚠ	ᛒ	ᛟ	ᛖ	ᛇ
Algiz - Elk	Ansuz - Message	Berkana – Birch	Dagaz- Dawn	Ehwaz - Horse	Eihwaz - Yew
ᚡ	ᚷ	ᚺ	◇	|	ᛋ
Fehu – Cattle, wealth	Gebo - Gift	Hagalaz – Hail	Ingwaz – Fertility	Isa - Ice	Jera - Harvest
ᚲ	ᛚ	ᛗ	ᛏ	ᛟ	ᛈ
Kenaz - torch	Laguz - Lake	Mannaz – Man	Nauthiz - Needs	Othala - Heritage	Pertho - Destiny
ᚱ	ᛋ	ᚦ	ᛏ	ᚢ	ᚹ
Raidho -Journey	Sowilo – Sun	Thurisaz - Mallet/giant	Tiwaz- Victory	Uruz - Ox	Wunjo – Joy

Question Asked:

Interpretation of the Reading

When drawn upright, place a checkmark above each rune drawn.
When drawn inverted, simply mark below the rune.

Algiz - Elk	Ansuz - Message	Berkana – Birch	Dagaz- Dawn	Ehwaz - Horse	Eihwaz - Yew
Fehu – Cattle, wealth	Gebo - Gift	Hagalaz – Hail	Ingwaz – Fertility	Isa - Ice	Jera - Harvest
Kenaz - torch	Laguz - Lake	Mannaz – Man	Nauthiz - Needs	Othala - Heritage	Pertho - Destiny
Raidho -Journey	Sowilo – Sun	Thurisaz Mallet/gia nt	Tiwaz- Victory	Uruz - Ox	Wunjo – Joy

Question Asked:

Interpretation of the Reading

Date: __/ __/ _____

When drawn upright, place a checkmark above each rune drawn.
When drawn inverted, simply mark below the rune.

Algiz - Elk	Ansuz - Message	Berkana – Birch	Dagaz- Dawn	Ehwaz - Horse	Eihwaz - Yew
Fehu – Cattle, wealth	Gebo - Gift	Hagalaz – Hail	Ingwaz – Fertility	Isa - Ice	Jera - Harvest
Kenaz - torch	Laguz - Lake	Mannaz – Man	Nauthiz - Needs	Othala - Heritage	Pertho - Destiny
Raidho -Journey	Sowilo – Sun	Thurisaz Mallet/giant	Tiwaz- Victory	Uruz - Ox	Wunjo – Joy

Question Asked:

Interpretation of the Reading

Date: __/ __/ _____

When drawn upright, place a checkmark above each rune drawn.
When drawn inverted, simply mark below the rune.

Algiz - Elk	Ansuz - Message	Berkana – Birch	Dagaz- Dawn	Ehwaz - Horse	Eihwaz - Yew
Fehu – Cattle, wealth	Gebo - Gift	Hagalaz – Hail	Ingwaz – Fertility	Isa - Ice	Jera - Harvest
Kenaz - torch	Laguz - Lake	Mannaz – Man	Nauthiz - Needs	Othala - Heritage	Pertho - Destiny
Raidho -Journey	Sowilo – Sun	Thurisaz Mallet/giant	Tiwaz- Victory	Uruz - Ox	Wunjo – Joy

Question Asked:

Interpretation of the Reading

When drawn upright, place a checkmark above each rune drawn.
When drawn inverted, simply mark below the rune.

Algiz - Elk	Ansuz - Message	Berkana – Birch	Dagaz- Dawn	Ehwaz - Horse	Eihwaz - Yew
Fehu – Cattle, wealth	Gebo - Gift	Hagalaz – Hail	Ingwaz – Fertility	Isa - Ice	Jera - Harvest
Kenaz - torch	Laguz - Lake	Mannaz – Man	Nauthiz - Needs	Othala - Heritage	Pertho - Destiny
Raidho -Journey	Sowilo – Sun	Thurisaz Mallet/gia nt	Tiwaz- Victory	Uruz - Ox	Wunjo – Joy

Question Asked:

Interpretation of the Reading

Date: __/ __/ _____

When drawn upright, place a checkmark above each rune drawn.
When drawn inverted, simply mark below the rune.

Algiz - Elk	Ansuz - Message	Berkana – Birch	Dagaz- Dawn	Ehwaz - Horse	Eihwaz - Yew
Fehu – Cattle, wealth	Gebo - Gift	Hagalaz – Hail	Ingwaz – Fertility	Isa - Ice	Jera - Harvest
Kenaz - torch	Laguz - Lake	Mannaz – Man	Nauthiz - Needs	Othala - Heritage	Pertho - Destiny
Raidho -Journey	Sowilo – Sun	Thurisaz Mallet/gia nt	Tiwaz- Victory	Uruz - Ox	Wunjo – Joy

Question Asked:

Interpretation of the Reading

Date: ___/ ___/ _____

When drawn upright, place a checkmark above each rune drawn.
When drawn inverted, simply mark below the rune.

�algiz	ᚨ	ᛒ	ᛞ	ᛖ	ᛇ
Algiz - Elk	Ansuz - Message	Berkana – Birch	Dagaz- Dawn	Ehwaz - Horse	Eihwaz - Yew
ᚠ	ᚷ	ᚺ	◇	ᛁ	ᛃ
Fehu – Cattle, wealth	Gebo - Gift	Hagalaz – Hail	Ingwaz – Fertility	Isa - Ice	Jera - Harvest
ᚲ	ᛚ	ᛗ	ᛏ	ᛟ	ᛈ
Kenaz - torch	Laguz - Lake	Mannaz – Man	Nauthiz - Needs	Othala - Heritage	Pertho - Destiny
ᚱ	ᛋ	ᚦ	ᛏ	ᚢ	ᚹ
Raidho -Journey	Sowilo – Sun	Thurisaz Mallet/gia nt	Tiwaz- Victory	Uruz - Ox	Wunjo – Joy

Question Asked:

Interpretation of the Reading

When drawn upright, place a checkmark above each rune drawn.
When drawn inverted, simply mark below the rune.

Algiz - Elk	Ansuz - Message	Berkana – Birch	Dagaz- Dawn	Ehwaz - Horse	Eihwaz - Yew
Fehu – Cattle, wealth	Gebo - Gift	Hagalaz – Hail	Ingwaz – Fertility	Isa - Ice	Jera - Harvest
Kenaz - torch	Laguz - Lake	Mannaz – Man	Nauthiz - Needs	Othala - Heritage	Pertho - Destiny
Raidho -Journey	Sowilo – Sun	Thurisaz Mallet/gia nt	Tiwaz- Victory	Uruz - Ox	Wunjo – Joy

Question Asked:

Interpretation of the Reading

Date: __/ __/ _____

When drawn upright, place a checkmark above each rune drawn.
When drawn inverted, simply mark below the rune.

Algiz - Elk	Ansuz - Message	Berkana – Birch	Dagaz- Dawn	Ehwaz - Horse	Eihwaz - Yew
Fehu – Cattle, wealth	Gebo - Gift	Hagalaz – Hail	Ingwaz – Fertility	Isa - Ice	Jera - Harvest
Kenaz - torch	Laguz - Lake	Mannaz – Man	Nauthiz - Needs	Othala - Heritage	Pertho - Destiny
Raidho -Journey	Sowilo – Sun	Thurisaz Mallet/giant	Tiwaz- Victory	Uruz - Ox	Wunjo – Joy

Question Asked:

Interpretation of the Reading

When drawn upright, place a checkmark above each rune drawn.
When drawn inverted, simply mark below the rune.

ᛉ	ᚠ	ᛒ	ᛞ	ᛗ	ᛃ
Algiz - Elk	Ansuz - Message	Berkana – Birch	Dagaz- Dawn	Ehwaz - Horse	Eihwaz - Yew
ᚡ	ᚷ	ᚺ	◇	ᛁ	ᛄ
Fehu – Cattle, wealth	Gebo - Gift	Hagalaz – Hail	Ingwaz – Fertility	Isa - Ice	Jera - Harvest
ᚲ	ᛚ	ᛗ	ᛏ	ᛟ	ᛈ
Kenaz - torch	Laguz - Lake	Mannaz – Man	Nauthiz - Needs	Othala - Heritage	Pertho - Destiny
ᚱ	ᛋ	ᚦ	ᛏ	ᚢ	ᚹ
Raidho -Journey	Sowilo – Sun	Thurisaz Mallet/gia nt	Tiwaz- Victory	Uruz - Ox	Wunjo – Joy

Question Asked:

Interpretation of the Reading

When drawn upright, place a checkmark above each rune drawn.
When drawn inverted, simply mark below the rune.

Algiz - Elk	Ansuz - Message	Berkana – Birch	Dagaz- Dawn	Ehwaz - Horse	Eihwaz - Yew
Fehu – Cattle, wealth	Gebo - Gift	Hagalaz – Hail	Ingwaz – Fertility	Isa - Ice	Jera - Harvest
Kenaz - torch	Laguz - Lake	Mannaz – Man	Nauthiz - Needs	Othala - Heritage	Pertho - Destiny
Raidho -Journey	Sowilo – Sun	Thurisaz Mallet/giant	Tiwaz- Victory	Uruz - Ox	Wunjo – Joy

Question Asked:

Interpretation of the Reading

Date: __/ __/ _____

When drawn upright, place a checkmark above each rune drawn.
When drawn inverted, simply mark below the rune.

Algiz - Elk	Ansuz - Message	Berkana – Birch	Dagaz- Dawn	Ehwaz - Horse	Eihwaz - Yew
Fehu – Cattle, wealth	Gebo - Gift	Hagalaz – Hail	Ingwaz – Fertility	Isa - Ice	Jera - Harvest
Kenaz - torch	Laguz - Lake	Mannaz – Man	Nauthiz - Needs	Othala - Heritage	Pertho - Destiny
Raidho -Journey	Sowilo – Sun	Thurisaz Mallet/giant	Tiwaz- Victory	Uruz - Ox	Wunjo – Joy

Question Asked:

Interpretation of the Reading

Date: __/ __/ _____

When drawn upright, place a checkmark above each rune drawn.
When drawn inverted, simply mark below the rune.

Algiz - Elk	Ansuz - Message	Berkana – Birch	Dagaz- Dawn	Ehwaz - Horse	Eihwaz - Yew
Fehu – Cattle, wealth	Gebo - Gift	Hagalaz – Hail	Ingwaz – Fertility	Isa - Ice	Jera - Harvest
Kenaz - torch	Laguz - Lake	Mannaz – Man	Nauthiz - Needs	Othala - Heritage	Pertho - Destiny
Raidho -Journey	Sowilo – Sun	Thurisaz Mallet/giant	Tiwaz- Victory	Uruz - Ox	Wunjo – Joy

Question Asked:

Interpretation of the Reading

Date: ___/ ___/ _____

When drawn upright, place a checkmark above each rune drawn.
When drawn inverted, simply mark below the rune.

Algiz - Elk	Ansuz - Message	Berkana – Birch	Dagaz- Dawn	Ehwaz - Horse	Eihwaz - Yew
Fehu – Cattle, wealth	Gebo - Gift	Hagalaz – Hail	Ingwaz – Fertility	Isa - Ice	Jera - Harvest
Kenaz - torch	Laguz - Lake	Mannaz – Man	Nauthiz - Needs	Othala - Heritage	Pertho - Destiny
Raidho -Journey	Sowilo – Sun	Thurisaz Mallet/giant	Tiwaz- Victory	Uruz - Ox	Wunjo – Joy

Question Asked:

Interpretation of the Reading

When drawn upright, place a checkmark above each rune drawn.
When drawn inverted, simply mark below the rune.

ᛉ	ᚨ	ᛒ	ᛞ	ᛗ	ᛇ
Algiz - Elk	Ansuz - Message	Berkana – Birch	Dagaz- Dawn	Ehwaz - Horse	Eihwaz - Yew
ᚠ	ᚷ	ᚺ	ᛝ	ᛁ	ᛃ
Fehu – Cattle, wealth	Gebo - Gift	Hagalaz – Hail	Ingwaz – Fertility	Isa - Ice	Jera - Harvest
ᚲ	ᛚ	ᛗ	ᚾ	ᛟ	ᛈ
Kenaz - torch	Laguz - Lake	Mannaz – Man	Nauthiz - Needs	Othala - Heritage	Pertho - Destiny
ᚱ	ᛋ	ᚦ	ᛏ	ᚢ	ᚹ
Raidho -Journey	Sowilo – Sun	Thurisaz Mallet/giant	Tiwaz- Victory	Uruz - Ox	Wunjo – Joy

Question Asked:

Interpretation of the Reading

When drawn upright, place a checkmark above each rune drawn.
When drawn inverted, simply mark below the rune.

Algiz - Elk	Ansuz - Message	Berkana – Birch	Dagaz- Dawn	Ehwaz - Horse	Eihwaz - Yew
Fehu – Cattle, wealth	Gebo - Gift	Hagalaz – Hail	Ingwaz – Fertility	Isa - Ice	Jera - Harvest
Kenaz - torch	Laguz - Lake	Mannaz – Man	Nauthiz - Needs	Othala - Heritage	Pertho - Destiny
Raidho -Journey	Sowilo – Sun	Thurisaz Mallet/gia nt	Tiwaz- Victory	Uruz - Ox	Wunjo – Joy

Question Asked:

Interpretation of the Reading

www.ingramcontent.com/pod-product-compliance
Lightning Source LLC
Chambersburg PA
CBHW071500070426
42452CB00041B/1945

* 9 780934 523707 *